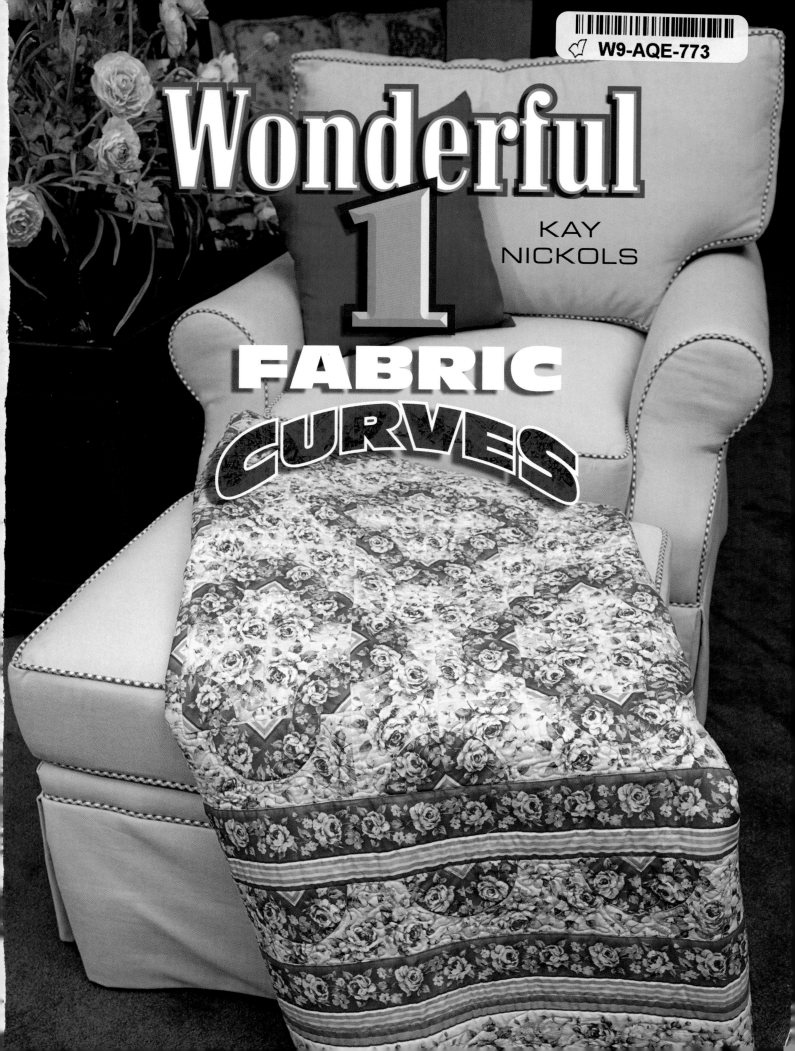

Wonderful

1

KAY NICKOLS

FABRIC

CURVES

Located in Paducah, Kentucky, the American Quilter's Society (AQS) is dedicated to promoting the accomplishments of today's quilters. Through its publications and events, AQS strives to honor today's quiltmakers and their work and to inspire future creativity and innovation in quiltmaking.

EXECUTIVE BOOK EDITOR: ANDI MILAM REYNOLDS
COPY EDITOR: CHRYSTAL ABHALTER
GRAPHIC DESIGN: ELAINE WILSON
LAYOUT DIAGRAMS: LYNDA SMITH AND ELAINE WILSON
COVER DESIGN: MICHAEL BUCKINGHAM
PHOTOGRAPHY: CHARLES R. LYNCH

Additional copies of this book may be ordered from the American Quilter's Society, PO Box 3290, Paducah, KY 42002-3290, or online at www.AmericanQuilter.com.

Text © 2011, Author, Kay Nickols
Artwork © 2011, American Quilter's Society

Library of Congress Cataloging-in-Publication Data

Nickols, Kay.
  Wonderful 1 fabric curves / by Kay Nickols.
    p. cm.
  Includes bibliographical references.
  ISBN 978-1-57432-647-5
  1. Patchwork--Patterns. 2. Quilting--Patterns. I. Title. II. Title:
Wonderful one fabric curves.
  TT835.N4943 2011
   746.46--dc23

                              2011017080

COVER: SPRING SONG, detail. Full quilt on page 65.

TITLE PAGE: TAPESTRY ROSE, detail. Full quilt on page 66.

Dedication

To the Almighty for showing me a curved path to quilt.

To my students for their creative works.

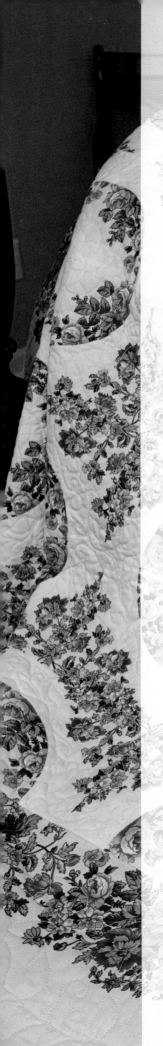

Acknowledgments

This book was brought about by the encouragement of Virginia Walton, one of the best curved piecing teachers.

Sincere thanks to AQS executive book editor, Andi Reynolds, for being so supportive of this refreshing idea in the quilt world. Also thanks to Charles R. Lynch for the fine photography, and Elaine Wilson and Michael Buckingham for the graphics and cover, respectively. A special thank you to the late Marge Boyle, sales and marketing director.

I humbly thank the quilters who have been kind enough to share their quilting talents with me. They are Elizabeth Ballard; Irene Blanchard; Kathy Blomfield; Nancy Boyce; Kathleen Clark; Helen Cole; SueAnn Cole; Vernita Dailey; Deborah Feldpausch; Carolyn Fox; Jan Gagliano; Deborah Gould; Robyn House-Guettler; Mary Haushauer; Nancy Hehrer; Dorothy D. Jones; Theresa Krieger; Ursula Kunkel; Deborah Lengkeek; Christine McEnhill; Margaret Metler; Arline Minsky; Louise Mueller; Susan Myers; Joyce Putnam, PhD; Kelly Sattler; Heather Spotts; Margaret Stiffler; Geraldine VanAgen; Nancy VanConant; and Stella Wilcox.

The following groups and quilt shops were most helpful as the book was developed:
Around the Block Quilt Shop, Portland, Michigan
Capital City Quilt Guild, Lansing, Michigan
Country Stitches, East Lansing, Michigan
Custom Quilts and Sewing, Haslett, Michigan
Everlasting Stitches, Holt, Michigan
Foster Friday Group
Lansing Area Patchers, Lansing, Michigan
Lunch Bunch
Material Girls
Piecemakers Quilt Guild, Saginaw, Michigan
Quilted Cottage, Saginaw, Michigan
Shiawassee Quilters, Owosso, Michigan
Yards of Fabric, Mason, Michigan
West Michigan Quilt Guild, Grand Rapids, Michigan

Special thanks to Higdon McBride Furniture Store, Paducah, Kentucky, and Karen and Johnny Weaver, Paducah, Kentucky, for photo settings.

THIS PAGE AND OPPOSITE: HUGS AND KISSES, detail. Full quilt on page 53.

Contents

OPPOSITE: LACE TRELLIS, detail. Full quilt on page 54.

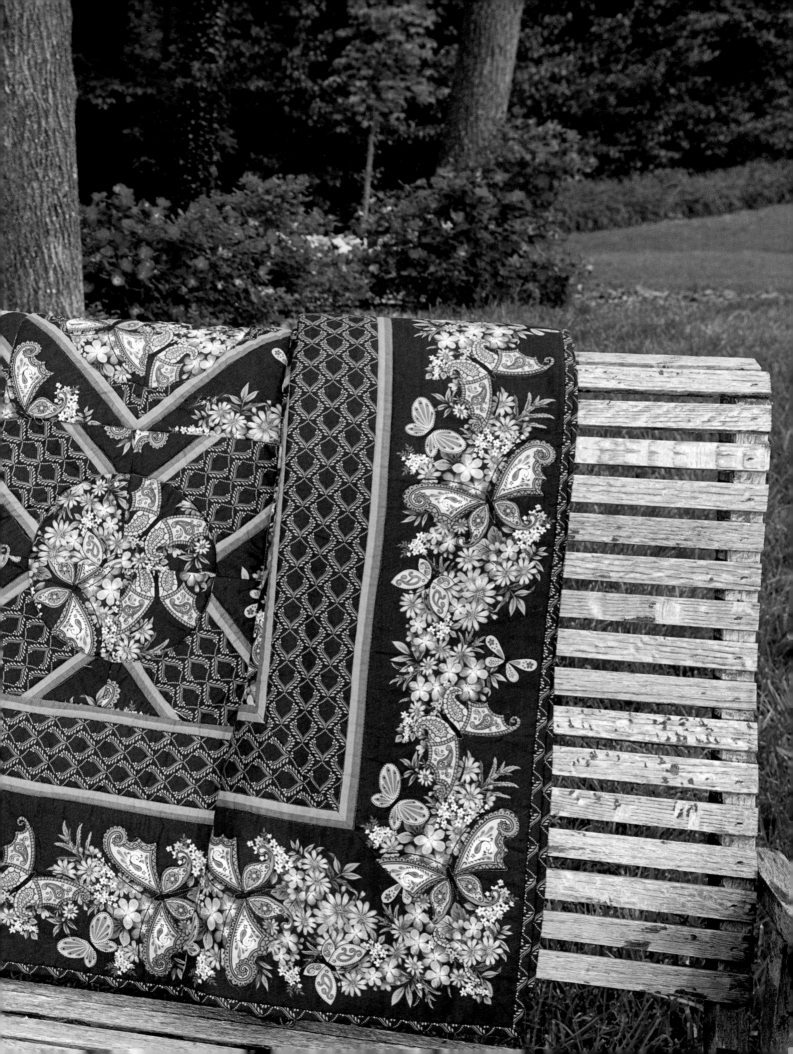

Preface

I enjoy making unique quilts and have found a way to use an old favorite—the curved, two-piece unit called the Drunkard's Path—and just one fabric to make a whole quilt top.

This curved-piecing process is another great way to use those wonderful fabrics that have a striped motif. For years, designers have created striped fabrics with lovely florals and fun novelty prints. Many times these fabrics are admired but not used. This is because there are too many design elements, often directional, and it is hard to visualize the fabrics in a finished quilt.

I find the use of only one such fabric gives me the advantages of (1) not having to shop for coordinating fabrics, and (2) creating a one-of-a-kind quilt. Shopping for that one, beautiful, striped fabric for the whole quilt top is a delightful challenge.

I am always surprised at the amazing results that I create as I work my Drunkard's Path units into a variety of intricate placements. I am sure you, too, will be amazed at the variety of looks that you will create from one fabric.

You will see many diverse ideas shown in the pictures of the quilts constructed by my students and me. Join in the pleasure of making a one-of-a-kind curved pieced quilt with one fabric. Make the fabric work for you!

Stitch a smile into every piece,

Kay

How to Use This Book

Working with only one striped fabric means your results will be unique, so there are no specific project instructions to make the quilts in this book.

Instead, I've told you everything you need to know to explore and create and have fun on your own making 1-fabric quilts with Drunkard's Path units:

○ Read the book and study the layout diagrams for the 27 quilts shown for ideas and inspiration (diagrams begin on page 41).

○ Go shopping, realizing that you may not find any of the exact fabrics in this book or from the manufacturers mentioned; it will be an adventure! A treasure hunt!

○ You will find it easiest to make clear templates of several sizes and carry them with you to choose and purchase a single striped fabric. The size of the motifs and distance between repeats will affect which size template will yield the best result and the yardage needed for the size of quilt you wish to make. Templates are on pages 69–77.

○ Ask the quilt shop staff for help in figuring yardage (hint: use the guidelines on page 8 to help them help you).

○ Use paper copies to determine the best way to cut your fabric (see page 25).

○ Cut and arrange pieces using a design wall (see page 25).

○ Follow the no-pin curved piecing technique and border and finishing techniques to create your unique quilt (see page 28).

OPPOSITE: PANDEMONIUM, detail. Full quilt on pages 56.

Shopping

Shopping for quilt fabric is always fun and sometimes challenging. Fabric to buy for 1-fabric curved piecing should have stripes with at least a ½" difference in width. Look for stripes with interest and high contrast. You will find florals, novelty prints, geometric designs mixed with animals, earth elements, and more. Stripes can run vertically or horizontally.

Look for the very best quality fabric to get the most reliable cuts. It is very disappointing to find that the design is misprinted on the fabric. Misprinted fabrics make consistent cuts virtually impossible.

Piecing curved units using one high quality striped fabric has an advantage since the weave is consistent and allows the two pieces of each unit to be sewn together without stretching either the concave or convex cuts. Quilters have difficulty when piecing together two fabrics such as loosely woven and tightly woven pieces. They will not lie flat and require more handling. When using just one fabric there is no need to pin two pieces together or clip the curves.

Quantity
- 4 yards of fabric will make a nice-sized wallhanging.
- A lap-size quilt requires 6 yards.
- A queen size requires at least 8 yards when making random cuts on the stripes.
- Fussy cuts for all quilt sizes will require at least 2 more yards.

- To achieve the look of the quilts in this book, borders and binding are also cut from this yardage.
- Purchase additional fabric for backing.

Stripe Types
Juvenile, novelty, and motif-stripe fabrics generally run horizontally. These fabrics are most often located in the juvenile print sections of quilt shops. Sometimes they are found in the decorator prints section. There are usually a variety of elements in the motifs (Fig. 1–1).

Fig. 1–1

I consider vertical striped prints to be wallpaper prints. They are generally composed of motifs that alternate florals and stripes. They sometimes have a high contrast background and then floral stripes. These are great for showing curved lines and have a soft or Victorian look in the finished quilt (Figs. 1–2 and 1–3).

The width of the stripe determines the template size (Figs. 1–4 and 1–5).

Fig. 1–2

Fussy-Cutting Stripes

Sometimes there are motifs in the stripes of the print that you do not want to use. Often they are a color or motif that detracts from the more desirable parts of the print. You just eliminate that part of the fabric you dislike for the Drunkard's Path units and use it elsewhere, so go ahead and buy that fabric if most of it speaks to you.

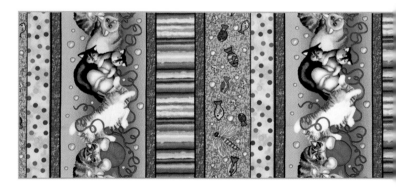

Fig. 1–3

Do Use These Fabrics

Curved-piece units like Drunkard's Path require stripes that are different but repetitive in width size, i.e., one is 3" and the other 4¼" as they alternate across the fabric. See the example in figure 1–6, page 10.

Fig. 1–4

Fabrics used in the quilts in this book are from some of my favorite designers. Jackie Robinson, a designer for Maywood Studio, creates split stripes as shown in the examples in figures 1–7a–f, page 10, as well as figure 1–2. Note how the stripe in each sample is set against both the light and the dark backgrounds, so it's split. Her designs are high in contrast and are wide enough to allow multiple cuts for extensive designs.

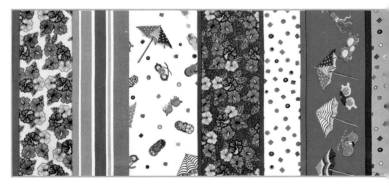

Fig. 1–5

Fig. 1–6

Fig. 1–7a. Maywood Studio

Fig. 1–7b

Fig. 1–7c

Fig. 1–7d

Fig. 1–7e

Fig. 1–7f

The Benartex Corporation has many stripes offered each season; an example is shown in figure 1-8a. Jinny Beyer, designing for RJR Fabrics, often creates high contrast and consistent stripe widths that provide great opportunities to create unique quilts, as shown in figure 1-8b.

Novelty fabrics good for the 1-fabric, curved-quilt process are also manufactured by South Sea Imports, Red Rooster Fabrics and Blank Textiles are shown in figures 1–8c–e.

Fig. 1–8a. Benartex

Fig. 1–8b. Jinny Beyer for RJR Fabrics

Fig. 1–8c. South Sea Imports

Fig. 1–8d. Red Rooster Fabrics

Fig. 1–8e. Blank Textiles

Shopping

Fig. 1–9a

Fig. 1–9b

Fig. 1–10

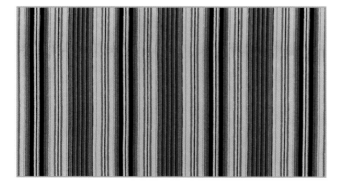

Fig. 1–11

Remember, fabric lines change constantly and are usually not available for very long, so you may not find any of the fabrics in this book available, but more importantly, when you see a striped fabric you like, buy it! And buy more than you think you will need!

A variety of template sizes are included for the 2-piece units of the Drunkard's Path, which creates a square in any size. Use the size that best shows off your fabric's stripe. The templates, shown on pages 69–77, range from a 3" x 3" finished unit to an 8" x 8" finished unit in quarter- or half-inch increments. See figures 1–9a and b for examples of how differently units cut from one fabric can look.

> ### Terrific Tip
> Make several sizes of see-through templates and take them with you when shopping for fabric.

High contrast in the stripes offers and accentuates the effect of the curved piecing, as shown in figure 1–10.

Fabrics to Avoid Using

Large amounts of negative space in the stripes eliminates the curved-piecing effect, as do stripes that are narrow, too even, or too busy. See figures 1–11 and 1–12.

Fig. 1–12

Fabrics that are of the same value have very low contrast; the curved piecing does not show. Figure 1–13 shows a fabric with stripes that have a nice variety in motifs, and good stripe widths, but are the same value even though there is a yellow background in one and blue in the other. If you put them in a copy machine on black and white, the two shades would show the same. The finished quilt would lose all movement of the curves and the design would be flat. Stripe widths that do not vary may yield spectacular designs but the curved-piecing effect is lost. Of course, you might like this look!

Fig. 1–13

BELOW: PANDEMONIUM, 98" x 98", made by Chris McEnhill, Grand Ledge, Michigan, and quilted by Robyn House-Guettler, Bay City, Michigan.

Shopping

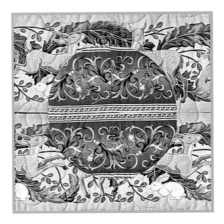

The final decision about using one fabric to make curved quilts is your choice. Both PANDEMONIUM, page 13, and DEER GOING IN CIRCLES are terrific quilts, even if they look quite different from the typical (is there such a thing?) 1-fabric curve quilt.

BELOW: DEER GOING IN CIRCLES, 57½" x 53½", made by Mary Hausauer, Owosso, Michigan, and quilted by Susan Myers, Haslett, Michigan.

Where to Find Striped Fabrics

Quality fabrics are found in quilt shops in your area. The owners have access to the latest fabric releases by quilt designers. These fabrics are not usually found in discount fabric stores, and it's always a good idea to support your local shop, since they are such a great source of assistance.

The discount fabric stores buy fabric flats or bolts at reduced prices from the manufacturers. These may be printed crookedly on the fabric, may be end runs, or not current releases. Some of the discount store fabrics are not a high quality weave and/or are loosely woven. All or any of these poor qualities in the fabrics can create frustration when cutting or sewing the curves accurately. The end result for the quilt is very disappointing.

Today quilters have a great advantage over former generations when shopping for fabric. The information age has increased shopping opportunities many times over. We can go online and shop directly from the manufacturers, designers, and retailers in other parts of the country. Special wholesalers who market fabrics that may have been discontinued are favorites for quilters. You can shop in the comfort of your home and have the fabrics delivered.

Shopping while on vacation or a business trip opens a new avenue for fabric surprises. There are fabric shops available in most countries of the world and terrific quilters, too. Local guides most generally can direct you. Telephone books, the Chamber of Commerce, and tourist information centers are other good sources.

Quilters shopping for 1-fabric curved quilts will find true treasures. You will never look at striped fabric the same way again. You will make the fabric work for you and be delightfully surprised with the results.

What If I Run Out of Fabric?

It is always wise to buy more fabric than you think you will need for a project, but what happens if you run out? Or perhaps you start another project and the leftover yardage is just what you need but you can't find more of it?

If you have planned the first project carefully and cut conservatively (see Cutting on page 21), you'll have more leftover fabric to work with. When the pieces become too small to make a complete patch, piece the patches together as shown in Figure 1–14. This approach is tried and true, found often in quilts from the nineteenth century.

Don't hesitate to cut your fabric in unexpected ways to create or complete borders, as shown in figure 3–1, page 20.

If piecing patches and borders together doesn't work for your project, use your design wall to scale it down (see Designing–Part 2 on page 29). The various sizes of templates in this book will help you do this successfully.

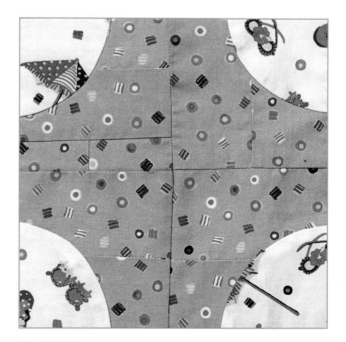

Fig. 1–14

Preparations

Fabric

I do not prewash my fabric. I also do not iron it because the stripe lines of the fabric designs are stretched ever so slightly when heat is applied. If there are wrinkles, I use a spray-on laundry product available that removes them—even bolt-fold wrinkles (see Resources on page 78). It is important to avoid any misalignments that can affect the cutting or sewing.

Design

It is important to use a design wall. The curved-piece blocks are so much easier to manipulate when they are on a wall. The creative eye will view new placements for more pleasing designs.

If you do not have a design wall, it's worthwhile to purchase an inexpensive table covering that has a flannel back. The flannel "grips" the pieces so they stay in place without pins. If you sew a hem at the bottom and insert a dowel, your "wall" may be rolled up out of the way.

Terrific Tip

Take your table cover design wall to classes and roll it up with pieces you may be working with when class ends. They will stay in place during transport home.

When you view your block placements from a distance, it might make a great difference in decisions for your final quilt design. A digital camera or a cell phone that takes photos are great tool options both to view your wall from a distance and to keep track of design ideas.

Templates

The curved-piecing process for 1-fabric quilts requires templates to make the old-fashioned Drunkard's Path pattern. Although available from many manufacturers, they may not have the sizes that fit your fabric's stripes.

To help you, I have included many template pattern sizes you can copy. I took my patterns to the local hardware person who fixes windows; he cut templates from heavy plexiglass. It was a minimal cost and it is great to have several sizes to take shopping before purchasing the fabric. Place the Drunkard's Path templates together on the fabric and slide them around until you get an effect you like (Figs. 2–1a–d, page 17).

Terrific Tip

Use any on-hand quilter's template material that you can see through to copy the templates. Then take them with you when you shop.

Fig. 2–1a

Fig. 2–1b

Fig. 2–1c

Fig. 2–1d

It is important to use a 28mm rotary cutter for cutting these curves. This smaller size rotary cutter cuts the angle of the curves more easily than larger cutters. A 28mm cutter fits most quilters' hands more comfortably and reduces stress on the hand, wrist, elbow, and shoulder.

You will be constructing units from a 3½" finished square up to a 7½" finished square, so it is important to have a variety of square rulers on hand for trimming and squaring. When the blocks are put together, some may be as large as 20" x 20". I use my 15" and 20" square rulers on a regular basis.

Tools

- ○ see-through template making material
- ○ ultra-fine permanent marker
- ○ 28mm rotary cutter with a NEW blade
- ○ cutting mat
- ○ 6" x 12" ruler
- ○ 4" to 20" square rulers
- ○ ¼" sewing machine foot (preferably not the one with a flange on edge) OR be able to move the needle to achieve a precise ¼" seam
- ○ stiletto (chop stick, orange stick, awl, or seam ripper) to manipulate fabric while sewing curves
- ○ neutral color thread
- ○ seam ripper
- ○ quilting pins
- ○ grips or tape for templates

Making the Quilt Top

Designing – Part 1

The Drunkard's Path unit is a time-honored quilters' favorite for design elements. The curves provide pleasing movement to the blocks and the overall finished quilt. These units provide infinite design possibilities as demonstrated in the quilts pictured throughout this book.

The very oldest block patterns made from these concave-plus-convex pieces have proven the test of time and gone by various names. Examples of traditional blocks are:

Fool's Puzzle
Baby Bunting
Mill Wheel
Love Ring
Chain Links
Snowball
King Tut's Crown
Doves

Jan Gagliano of Haslett, Michigan, constructed a sampler for teaching purposes using these blocks (see Figs. 3-1a–i, page 20). One fabric of novelty beach motifs was used to construct this teaching tool; see Fig. 3–2, page 20.

According to *Encyclopedia of Pieced Quilt Patterns* by Barbara Brackman (AQS, 1993), these names also describe patterns made with this unit (some are quite charming!):

Wanderer's Path in the Wilderness
Crazy Quilt
Wonder of the World
Robbing Peter to Pay Paul
Solomon's Puzzle
Drunkard's Rail
Old Maid's Puzzle
Endless Trail
Crooked Path
Country Cousin
World's Wonder
Boston Trail
The Pumpkin Vine

And there are still other traditional blocks made from this unit. Many of my students have combined some of the traditional blocks with original settings to make dynamic quilts.

When following traditional block settings, be careful to place the units in the prescribed position. If one of the units is turned incorrectly in the block, it may not be noticed until the quilt top is completed. (This is where a design wall comes in handy.) Look closely at the four corners of SERENDIPITY, page 19. Still lovely, isn't it!

Terrific Tip

Purchase a door peep-hole at a hardware store to view the quilt layout "at a distance" for a fast and easy check of unit placement.

SERENDIPITY, 80" x 96", made by Dorothy Jones, Lansing, Michigan, and quilted by Robyn House-Guettler, Bay City, Michigan.

Fig. 3–1a–i. BEACH PARTY, 52" x 54", made by Jan Gagliano, Haslett, Michigan.

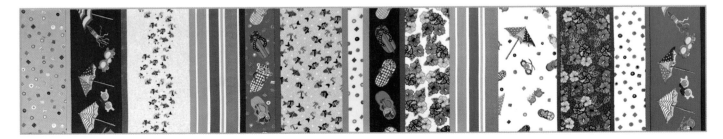

Fig. 3–2. Novelty fabric used in BEACH PARTY teaching sampler.

Wonderful 1 FABRIC CURVES ○ Kay Nickols

Cutting

Before cutting, open the fabric to see if the selvage edges are printed the same. If they are not, you must decide which side of the print will have the most cuts for the color and scale of the motifs to be used. This is the best time to measure the width of each motif stripe. You should have a minimum of two widths to fit either the convex or concave templates (see Fig. 3–3a–d).

The split striped fabric pictured in Figs.1–9a and 1–9b on page 12 are excellent examples of the multiple cuts that can be made with wide stripes but only two stripe colors, blue/cream. Fabrics like this one offer the most design options.

Fig. 3–3a

Fig. 3–3b

Terrific Tip

Place fabric on a copy machine and cut paper pieces from the copies. Play with different paper cuts along the design before actually cutting into the fabric.

All of the quilts shown were made from motifs that had been fussy cut. Fussy cuts have the clear templates placed on the stripe in exactly the same place for each cut or to showcase different specific motifs (think "I Spy" quilts). This method is often used to accent a particular animal or flower. More fabric is required for fussy cutting, but the end results may be more satisfying for the finished quilt design.

The quite regular garlands and wreaths in AUTUMN ARBOR and POSIES AND LACE, page 22, were achieved by fussy cutting. Equally pretty, VICTORIAN CURVES, page 23, has more of a random look to it, fussy cut or not. CIRCLES OF JOY, page 23, on the other hand, cut randomly so that the circles seem to bounce and play, might not have been as joyful had it been fussy cut.

Fig. 3–3c

Fig. 3–3d

Making the Quilt Top

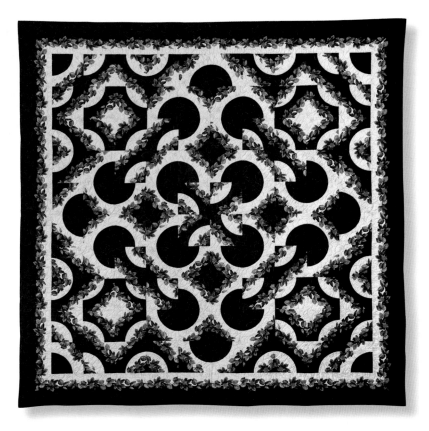

RIGHT: AUTUMN ARBOR, 82" x 82", made by Irene Blanchard, East Lansing, Michigan, and quilted by Robyn House-Guettler, Bay City, Michigan.

LEFT: POSIES AND LACE, 54" x 68", made by Margaret A. Stiffler, Holt, Michigan, and quilted by Susan Myers, Haslett, Michigan.

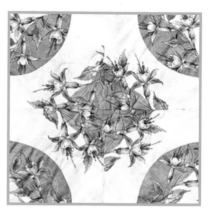

LEFT: VICTORIAN CURVES, 79" x 79", made and quilted by Margaret A. Stiffler, Holt, Michigan.

RIGHT: CIRCLES OF JOY, 80" x 80", made by Louise Mueller, East Lansing, Michigan, and quilted by Nancy Boyse, East Lansing, Michigan.

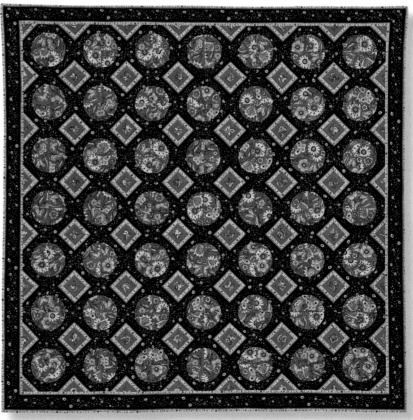

Making the Quilt Top

When the fabric is unfolded you can choose a favorite stripe to use as borders or the binding. Most often I complete a major part of the top and then audition border choices. If there is a lot of one color in the body of the piece, I might choose to eliminate it in the stripe/stripes used for a border. Sometimes I use a binding to match the border so there is a more of a softened edge to the quilt, as in CHINA PLATES.

BELOW: CHINA PLATES, 64" x 84", made by Carolyn Fox, Ionia, Michigan, and quilted by Stella Wilcox, Lake Odessa, Michigan

Terrific Tip

Make a window template from paper or cardboard if you don't have see-through template plastic.

Fig. 3–4. The same fabric in different colorways, designed by Bethany S. Reynolds, Blank Textiles.

Place the cuts, whether paper or fabric, in various arrangements of blocks on your design wall. Photograph each layout with a cell phone or digital camera before you rearrange it so you can find the most pleasing setting. An easy way to begin is to make 36 units to sew some traditional blocks (see Fig. 3–1 on page 20). It will be easy to deviate from these blocks to create more original settings.

Cut more pieces from different parts of the stripe if you think your arrangement does not have enough spark. Quilts created from the same fabric will look entirely different if cut from other portions of the same stripe (see Figs. 3–4 through 3–6).

Good examples of the same fabric in different colorways and designs are shown in Figs. 3–4, 3–5, and 3–6. Margaret A. Stiffler of Holt, Michigan, made the white background wallhanging. Deborah Lengkeek of St. Johns, Michigan, made the black background wallhanging.

Fig. 3–5. UNQUILTED TOP, 25½" x 25½" made by Margaret A. Stiffler, Holt, Michigan.

RIGHT: **Fig. 3–6.** UNQUILTED TOP, 38" x 38", made by Deborah Lengkeek, St. Johns, Michigan.

Making the Quilt Top

Throughout this book there are many quilts shown made from the same fabric, but the quilters had the fabric work for them in a variety of ways. Some used traditional blocks, some expanded traditional blocks, and others created new blocks. The possibilities are endless. See page 27 for a dramatic example of one fabric sewn into one 2-piece unit yielding four dramatically different quilts.

Buy lots of extra yardage and try lots of variations. You could even make a reversible quilt; use one side for fall and one for winter.

Always cut off the selvages before cutting strips, borders, and pieces.

Cut 2 strips 2" wide from the length of the fabric for the binding. If you are going to use a no-binding finish or front- or back-fold bindings, you do not need to cut binding strips.

When cutting the borders, be sure to measure the top first (horizontally and vertically through the center) and include ¼" seam allowances along both edges of the stripe motifs.

Terrific Tip

Some stripes that may not fit the design elements of the quilt you're working on can be used for future quilt creations. For example, they might be used as frames, sashing, or cornerstones.

Designing with one fabric can be a true adventure in your quilt world. Piecing with curves will make the adventure even more challenging and fun for you!

Terrific Tip

Always cut the convex and concave units from lengthwise strips instead of across the width of fabric so that there will be stripes left for border choices. If you cut across the stripes you reduce the choices for your borders.

Sewing

I was always apprehensive about piecing curves until I took a class from Virginia Walton, the creator of Creative Curves. She showed us how to sew curves without using pins.

Long-time quilting students in my classes were all very skeptical about the no-pin process, but after 10 minutes of practicing they began chain piecing curved Drunkard's Path units, pinless. While before they had always taken the time to pin the pieces, now they, too, were amazed with the ease in sewing the non-pinned units.

Follow these directions, and you will be amazed, too:

○ It is important to always sew a ¼" seam.

○ It helps to loosen the presser foot pressure because less is good for the ease of moving pieces as you stitch.

○ Also, it helps to use an open-toe ¼" foot.

○ If you have a needle-down option on your sewing machine it makes the process go even faster to keep the pieces aligned as you are always sewing a straight seam.

HOPE OF GLORY, 70" x 90", made by Kathy Blomfield, Grand Ledge, Michigan, and quilted by Susan Myers, Haslett, Michigan.

POINSETTIAS IN WINTER, 57" x 77", made by Deborah Feldpausch, Fowler, Michigan, and quilted by Susan Myers, Haslett, Michigan.

POINSETTIAS ON POINT, 54" x 70", made and quilted by Deborah Gould, Portland, Michigan.

WINTER MEDALLION, 72" x 72", made by Margaret Metler, Haslett, Michigan, and quilted by Susan Myers, Haslett, Michigan.

Align these corners exactly

Fig. 3–7

Fig. 3–8

Fig. 3–9

Piecing the Drunkard's Path Units (Fig. 3–7)

○ Place the convex (outside curve) piece right-side up.

○ Place the concave (inside curve) right-side down.

○ Align the top of the concave piece with the top straight edge of the convex curve piece.

This placement appears to be impossible to sew into a curved unit but it does and here is how:

○ **Do not pin** the pieces together in the middle (this will make putting the pieces together more difficult).

○ Place the aligned pieces under the presser foot.

○ Hang on to the needle and bobbin threads and sew three stitches along the concave curve.

○ When you have sewn the first three stitches, realign the edges to match and sew three more stitches.

○ Carefully bring the curved seams together (watch where the seam edges are coming together about ½" before the needle).

○ When you are halfway along the seam's length (at the midpoint of the curve), put the needle in the down position.

○ Hold the fabrics with a stiletto or a similar tool and realign the fabric pieces to continue to sew in a straight seam.

○ As you get near the end (the last seven stitches or so), draw in the concave piece to match the bottom edge of the convex piece and hold them in place with a stiletto.

○ Gently handle the two pieces to prevent stretching and inconsistent seams.

○ Do not heat press these units. The seam will tend to fall to either side. Once you see how the seam naturally falls, finger press the seam (Fig. 3–8, page 28).

○ Clipping curves is not necessary.

Again, I cannot stress enough that **there must always be a ¼" seam.**

Use practice pieces until you learn this tried-and-true process. In a very short time you will be chain piecing Drunkard's Path units without pinning. It may seem at times that there is a little pleat as you are sewing a seam, but when the two pieces are opened and finger-pressed, the pleat will disappear.

Designing – Part 2

It is best to begin designing your quilt using 36 Drunkard's Path units. The layout diagrams for the quilts shown in this book begin on page 42. There are four general layouts, with variations, and the diagrams are grouped that way. Remember that these are just suggestions, and your results will vary, based on your fabric choice.

FUCHSIA IN THE ROUND was designed using the traditional pattern called Snowball (See Fig. 3–9. page 28). The high contrast of the purple and cream stripe with the fuchsia blossoms created a modern look for a traditional block. The same cut units of the violets fabric were used in SPRING SONG, but the block placement created a nontraditional setting.

RIGHT: SPRING SONG, 66" x 66", made by Jan Gagliano, Haslett, Michigan, and quilted by Nancy Boyse, East Lansing, Michigan.

FUCHSIA IN THE ROUND, 62½" x 70½", made by the author and quilted by Nancy Boyse, East Lansing, Michigan.

Making the Quilt Top

RIGHT: MEDALLION DAISIES,
55" x 75½", made by the author
and quilted by Nancy Boyse, East
Lansing, Michigan.

LEFT: HUGS AND KISSES,
80" x 90", made by Deborah
Lengkeek, St. Johns, Michigan,
and quilted by Nancy Boyse, East
Lansing, Michigan.

Seven-inch square units were used in MEDALLION DAISIES, page 30. I created this original design by cutting different parts of the stripes to be able to make a variety of units.

One group of students was challenged to use the same fabric and make their design cuts to be different than each of the other quilters'. These students used the poinsettia, fuschia, butterflies, daisies, and blue/floral stripe fabrics to create one-of-a-kind quilts. See the quartet of poinsettia fabric quilts on page 27.

Another group was challenged to use the same two pieces throughout the construction of their quilts. These fabrics are the violets stripe in Jan Gagliano's SPRING SONG (see page 29), and multi-floral stripe in Deborah Lengkeek's HUGS AND KISSES, page 30. The pattern in HUGS AND KISSES is an old favorite Drunkard's Path block called Snowball.

The quilt made by Ursula Kunkel of Flushing, Michigan, BUTTERFLIES AND LACE, is another example of an old-timey Drunkard's Path pattern whose designs are pleasing to the eye when made with one fabric.

BUTTERFLIES AND LACE, 61" x 77", made by Ursula Kunkel and quilted by Missy O'Connor, both of Flushing, Michigan.

CATZ, 49" x 53", made by
Chris McEnhill, Grand Ledge,
Michigan.

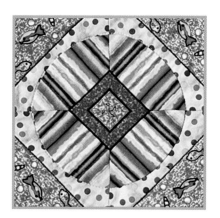

I have tried combining two different-sized units, for example, 7" finished template sets and 3½" finished template sets to make a medallion quilt. The larger 36-piece block is surrounded by the smaller blocks as a border. This is a challenging exercise but well worth the end result. Examples of a medallion quilt are SPRING SONG (see page 29) and MEDALLION DAISIES (see page 30). These are two variations and fun to try with other stripe fabrics. Even though MEDALLION DAISIES isn't quite symmetrical, the fabric is so pretty, you don't notice!

As you plan your design, watch the orientation of the blocks carefully. Chris McEnhill of Grand Ledge, Michigan, got very effective results with attention to placement of the stripes in CATZ.

Borders

There are many options for borders for 1-fabric, curved-pieced quilt tops. Since you have fabric stripes left, audition them against the top's edges on the design wall. Fold different parts of the fabric stripes, pin them next to the top and walk out of the room. When you return you will have an instant reaction to the correct feel for an overall finish. See how much more of an Asian feel the butted striped borders add to Sue Ann Cole's ORIENTAL CHRISTMAS ORNAMENTS, page 33.

LEFT: ORIENTAL CHRISTMAS ORNAMENTS, 65" x 73", made by Sue Ann Cole, Grand Ledge, Michigan, and quilted by Susan Myers, Haslett, Michigan.

Note what can happen with 1-fabric curved tops when the design blends into or makes up part of the border:

○ Arline Minsky of St. Johns, Michigan, trimmed the outer rows and columns of FUCHSIA PATHWAYS to stop and preserve her on-point, strippy design.

FUCHSIA PATHWAYS, 92" x 95", made by Arline Minsky, St. Johns, Michigan, and quilted by Nancy Boyse, East Lansing, Michigan.

Making the Quilt Top

RIGHT: GARDEN OF SUNFLOWERS, 60" x 79", made by Vernita Dailey, Okemos, Michigan, and quilted by Susan Myers, Haslett, Michigan.

LEFT: INDIA JEWEL, 38" x 53½", made by Kathleen Kelley Clark, Corunna, Michigan, and quilted by Susan Myers, Haslett, Michigan.

Wonderful 1 FABRIC CURVES ○ Kay Nickols

○ Vernita Dailey's design for GARDEN OF SUNFLOWERS, page 34, used Drunkard's Path units in a straight set to create an effective border.

○ The straightforward use of the stripe cut crosswise creates a true frame for INDIA JEWEL, page 34.

If the quilt top is a large bed quilt you may need a wider border that incorporates more than one stripe. If you're completing a wallhanging, only one stripe may be needed.

The mood of the top may inspire borders that may lighten or darken the overall look of the quilt. SERENDIPITY by Dorothy Jones of Lansing, Michigan, page 19, has a light, bright center, so the quilter balanced the look of the quilt with a dark stripe in the border. If your quilt tends to be dark in the center like Kelly Sattler's DAISY CHAIN, you may want to add a light stripe for the border.

Multiple borders can be quite striking, as in LACE TRELLIS, page 36. TAPESTRY ROSE, page 36, becomes a medallion quilt with so many different borders, all cut from one wonderful fabric.

When the light and dark are even in the design the border makes no difference in the mood of the piece. This happened with Stella Wilcox's UNCHAINED CHAIN LINKS, page 37, which has added interest by having some of the overall design extend into the border.

Most of the quilts shown have striped fabrics with floral motifs that look great when the borders are mitered, as in BUTTERFLIES AND LACE, detail, page 37. Some of the quilts have pieced corners that accentuate the stripe differences within the fabric.

DAISY CHAIN, 81" x 96", made by Kelly Sattler, DeWitt, Michigan, and quilted by Nancy Boyse, East Lansing, Michigan.

Making the Quilt Top

LEFT: LACE TRELLIS, 68" x 75½", made by Teresa Krieger, Saranac, Michigan, and quilted by Susan Myers, Haslett, Michigan.

RIGHT: TAPESTRY ROSE, 57" x 64", made by Elizabeth A. Ballard, Gaines, Michigan, and quilted by Susan Myers, Haslett, Michigan.

RIGHT: UNCHAINED CHAIN LINKS,
64" x 70", made and quilted
by Stella Wilcox, Lake Odessa,
Michigan.

LEFT: BUTTERFLIES AND LACE,
detail, made by Ursula Kunkel,
Flushing, Michigan and quilted
by Missy O'Connor, Flushing,
Michigan. Full quilt on page 31.

Making the Quilt Top

AROUND ABOUT TOBACCO ROAD has a scalloped border that adds a fine finish to the overall design of the quilt. Borders are like frosting on a cake; it's a matter of taste but necessary to complete the objective.

If you're using a layout diagram from this book, remember—the sky's the limit on adding borders! Your quilt top will speak to you, and you should listen to what it says.

BELOW: AROUND ABOUT TOBACCO ROAD, 74" x 96", made by Nancy Van Conant, Lansing, Michigan, and quilted by Stella Wilcox, Lake Odessa, Michigan.

Finishing

Quilting

The quilting designs used for most 1-fabric quilts are overall patterns or pantographs. This choice does not distract from the designs created by the curved pieces. Many quilters use invisible thread for the same reason. Others choose variegated thread to blend in with the motif colors, which leaves the pieced design elements of the quilt as the main focus.

There are a few quilts shown that have negative space in the piecing to show off some custom quilting designs, for example, vines and leaves to complement the floral motif fabric.

Binding

Many of the quilts have a reversible binding. This finish leaves a very clean look to the edges of the quilt. The binding on the back of the quilt matches the backing fabric, and the front has a portion of the top fabric to match the finished top.

To Make a Reversible Binding

- ○ Cut enough 1¼" width pieces of the backing fabric to make binding to go around the quilt.

- ○ Cut enough 1¼" width pieces of the front fabric to make binding to go around the quilt.

- ○ Sew these two newly constructed strips together to make a 2" wide binding.

- ○ Attach as you would any binding.

DAISY CHAIN, detail, made by Kelly Sattler, DeWitt, Michigan, and quilted by Nancy Boyse, East Lansing, Michigan. Full quilt on page 35.

Finishing

Sometimes I use a knife-edge finish on a quilt if I do not have binding fabric that suits the design of the border. This finish requires folding the back edge and front edge together to make a seam. It is best to trim away ¼" of the batting's edge so the turn is smooth and not bulky. I use a ladder stitch and invisible thread to hand finish the knife edge.

Generally, French-fold (double-fold) binding is used most often because it wears well. This is especially true when the quilt is a bed quilt that will be used on a daily basis.

Labeling

Label your one-of-a-kind, 1-fabric, curved-piece creation. Include the quiltmaker's name, the quilter, the location of each, and the date the quilt was completed. This documentation is very important when giving a quilt as a gift. The occasion for the gift and the recipient's name should be included as well.

LEFT: HOPE OF GLORY, detail, made by Kathy Blomfield, Grand Ledge, Michigan, and quilted by Susan Myers, Haslett, Michigan. Full quilt on page 27.

Drunkard's Path
Layout Diagrams

Autumn Arbor

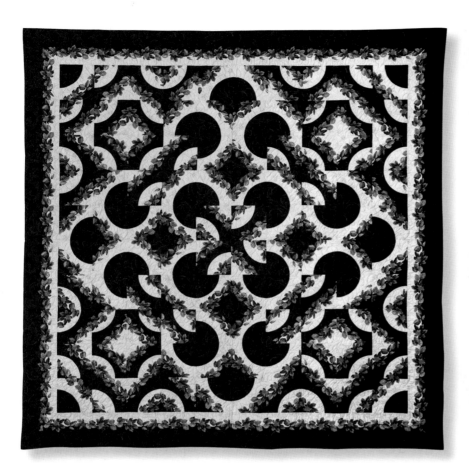

A

B

Autumn Arbor
82" x 82"
Made by Irene Blanchard,
East Lansing, Michigan
Quilted by Robyn House-
Guettler, Bay City, Michigan.
6½" templates on page 71.

GARDEN OF SUNFLOWERS

GARDEN OF SUNFLOWERS
60" x 79"
Made by Vernita Dailey,
Okemos, Michigan, and
quilted by Susan Myers,
Haslett, Michigan.
4¾" templates on page 75.

Victorian Curves

A

B

Victorian Curves
79" x 79"
Made and quilted by Margaret A.
Stiffler, Holt, Michigan.
5½" templates on page 72.

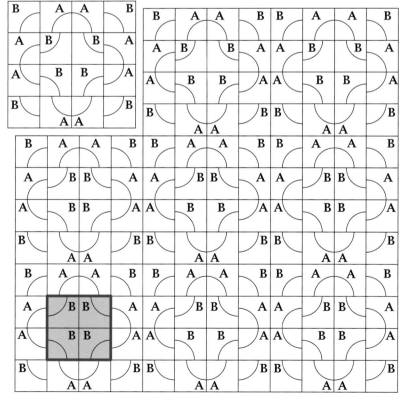

Wonderful 1 FABRIC CURVES ○ Kay Nickols

FUCHSIA PATHWAYS

A

B

FUCHSIA PATHWAYS
92" x 95"
Made by Arline Minsky,
St. Johns, Michigan, and
quilted by Nancy Boyse,
East Lansing, Michigan.
5¼" templates on page 73.

AROUND ABOUT TOBACCO ROAD

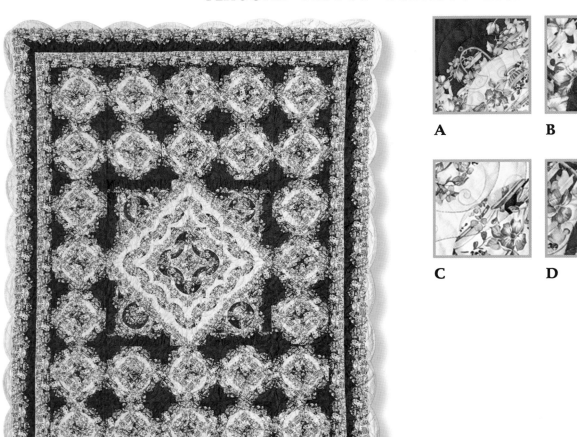

A   B

C   D

AROUND ABOUT TOBACCO
ROAD, 74" x 96"
Made by Nancy Van Conant,
Lansing, Michigan, and
quilted by Stella Wilcox,
Lake Odessa, Michigan.
3½" templates on page 76.

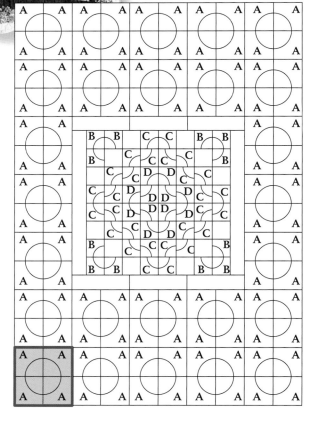

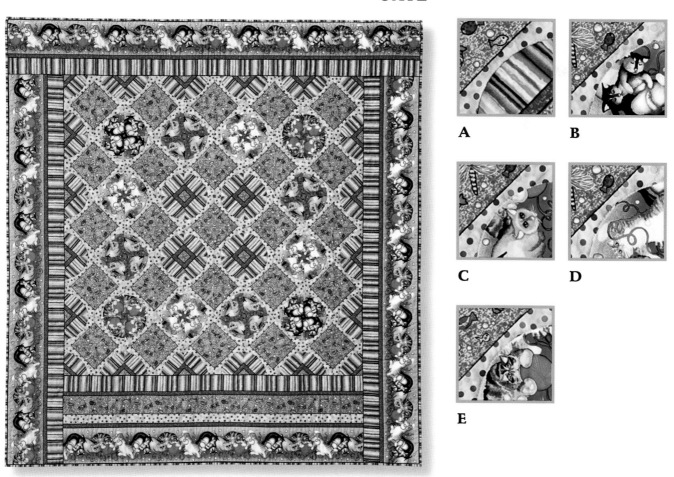

A B

C D

E

Catz, 49" x 53"
Made and quilted by
Chris McEnhill,
Grand Ledge, Michigan.
3½" templates on page 76.

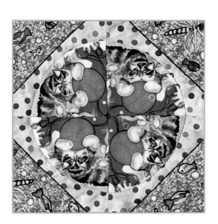

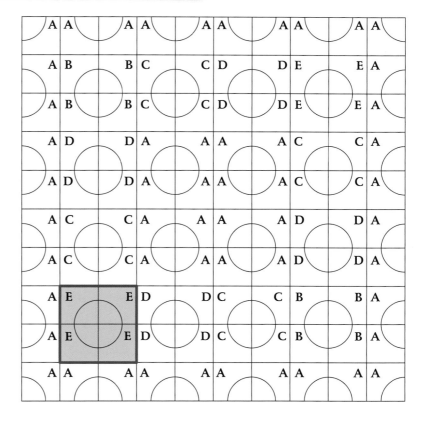

CHINA PLATES

A

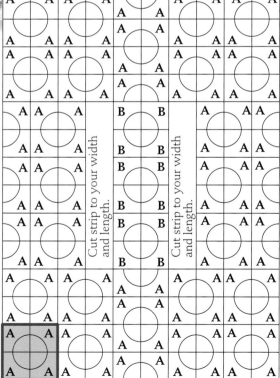

B

CHINA PLATES
64" x 84"
Made by Carolyn Fox,
Ionia, Michigan, and
quilted by Stella Wilcox,
Lake Odessa, Michigan.
4¾" templates on page 75.

CIRCLES OF JOY

CIRCLES OF JOY
80" x 80"
Made by Louise Mueller,
East Lansing, Michigan, and
quilted by Nancy Boyse,
East Lansing, Michigan.
5" templates on page 74.

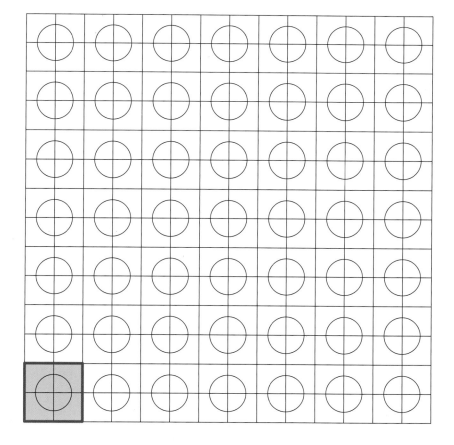

DAISY CHAIN

A

B

DAISY CHAIN
81" x 96"
Made by Kelly Sattler,
DeWitt, Michigan, and
quilted by Nancy Boyse,
East Lansing, Michigan.
7" templates on page 70.

DEER GOING IN CIRCLES

DEER GOING IN CIRCLES
57½" x 53½"
Made by Mary Hausauer,
Owosso, Michigan, and
quilted by Susan Myers,
Haslett, Michigan.
5" templates on page 74.

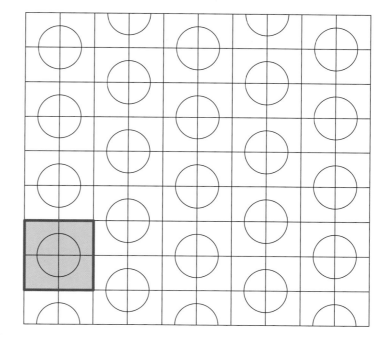

FUCHSIA IN THE ROUND

FUCHSIA IN THE ROUND
62½" x 70½"
Made by the author, and
quilted by Nancy Boyse,
East Lansing, Michigan.
4½" templates on page 76.

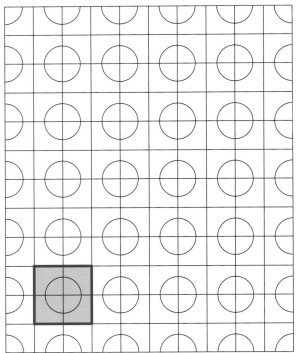

Wonderful 1 FABRIC CURVES ○ Kay Nickols

Hugs and Kisses

Hugs and Kisses
80" x 90"
Made by Deborah Lengkeek,
St. Johns, Michigan, and
quilted by Nancy Boyse,
East Lansing, Michigan.
5" templates on page 74.

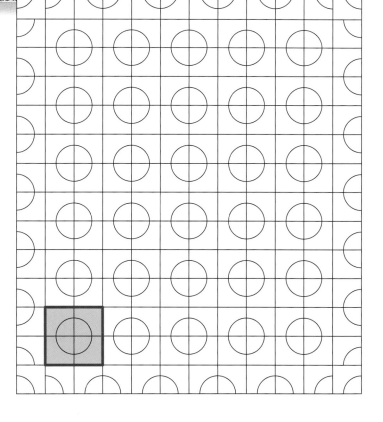

A

B

LACE TRELLIS
68" x 75½"
Made by Teresa Krieger,
Saranac, Michigan, and
quilted by Susan Myers,
Haslett, Michigan.
4¾" templates on page 75.

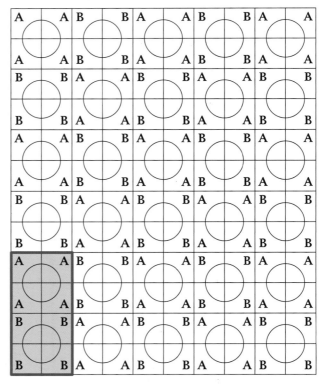

ORIENTAL CHRISTMAS ORNAMENTS

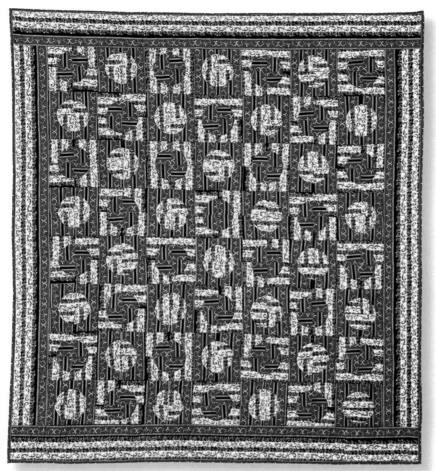

A

B

ORIENTAL CHRISTMAS
ORNAMENTS
65" x 73"
Made by Sue Ann Cole,
Grand Ledge, Michigan, and
quilted by Susan Myers,
Haslett, Michigan.
4" templates on page 77.

PANDEMONIUM

PANDEMONIUM
98" x 98"
Made by Chris McEnhill,
Grand Ledge, Michigan, and
quilted by Robyn House-Guettler,
Bay City, Michigan.
8" templates on page 69.

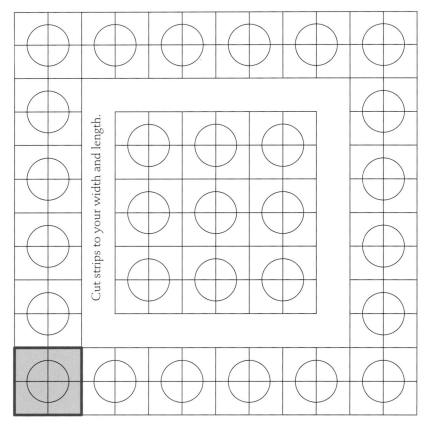

Cut strips to your width and length.

POINSETTIAS IN WINTER

POINSETTIAS IN WINTER
57" x 77"
Made by Deborah Feldpausch,
Fowler, Michigan, and
quilted by Susan Myers,
Haslett, Michigan.
5" templates on page 74.

POINSETTIAS ON POINT

A

B

C

POINSETTIAS ON POINT
54" x 70"
Made and quilted by Deborah
Gould, Portland, Michigan.
5" templates on page 74.

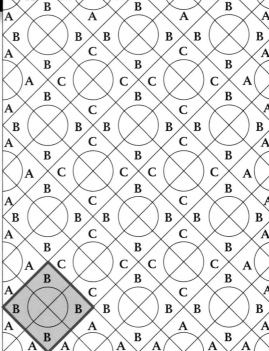

BUTTERFLIES AND LACE

A

B

BUTTERFLIES AND LACE
61" x 77"
Made by Ursula Kunkel,
Flushing, Michigan, and
quilted by Missy O'Connor,
Flushing, Michigan.
3½" templates on page 76.

HOPE OF GLORY

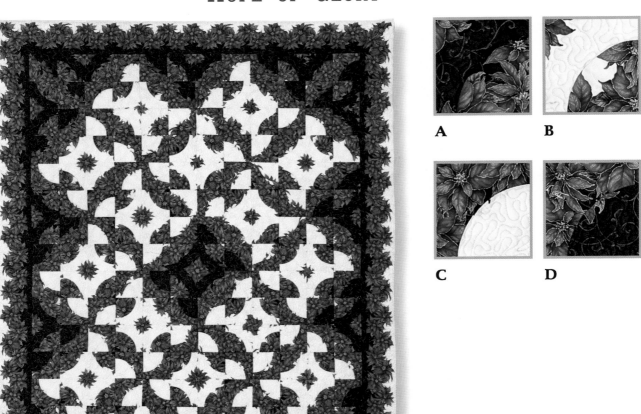

A **B**

C **D**

HOPE OF GLORY
70" x 90"
Made by Kathy Blomfield,
Grand Ledge, Michigan, and
quilted by Susan Myers,
Haslett, Michigan.
5" templates on page 74.

INDIA JEWEL

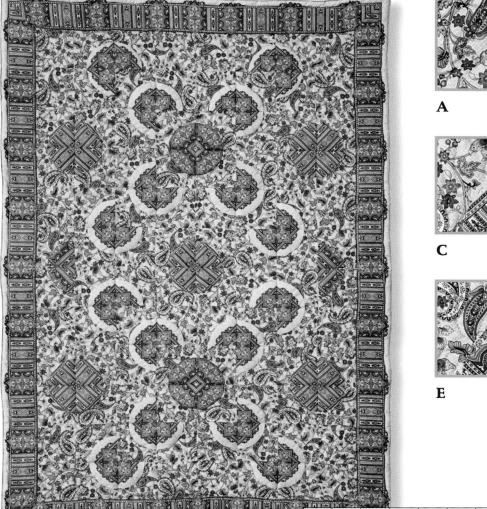

A   **B**

C   **D**

E

INDIA JEWEL
38" x 53½"
Made by Kathleen Kelley Clark,
Corunna, Michigan, and
quilted by Susan Myers,
Haslett, Michigan.
4" templates on page 77.

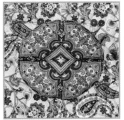

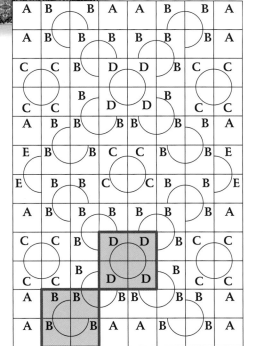

MEDALLION DAISIES

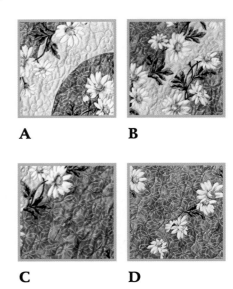

A   **B**

C   **D**

MEDALLION DAISIES
55" x 67½"
Made by the author and
quilted by Nancy Boyse,
East Lansing, Michigan.
7" templates on page 70.

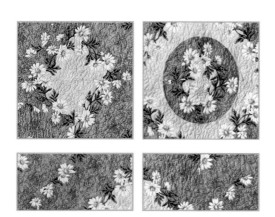

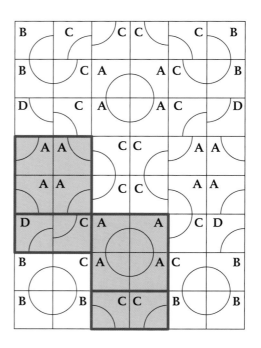

POSIES AND LACE

A

B

POSIES AND LACE
54" x 68"
Made by Margaret A. Stiffler,
Holt, Michigan, and
quilted by Susan Myers,
Haslett, Michigan.
3" templates on page 77.

SERENDIPITY

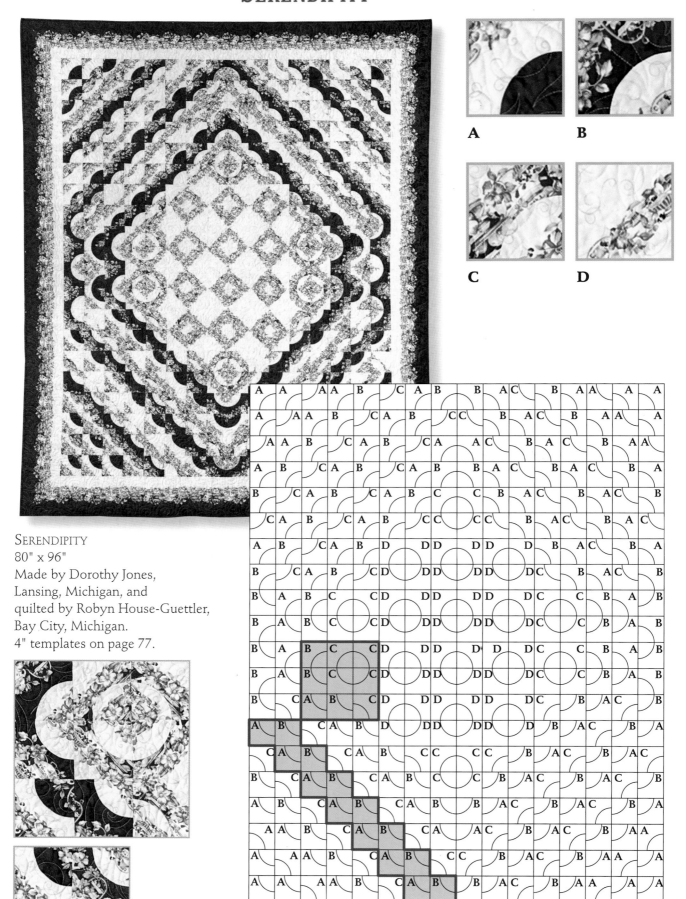

SERENDIPITY
80" x 96"
Made by Dorothy Jones,
Lansing, Michigan, and
quilted by Robyn House-Guettler,
Bay City, Michigan.
4" templates on page 77.

A   B

C   D

Wonderful 1 FABRIC CURVES ○ Kay Nickols

SPRING SONG

SPRING SONG
66" x 66"
Made by Jan Gagliano,
Haslett, Michigan, and
quilted by Nancy Boyse,
East Lansing, Michigan.
3" templates on page 77.

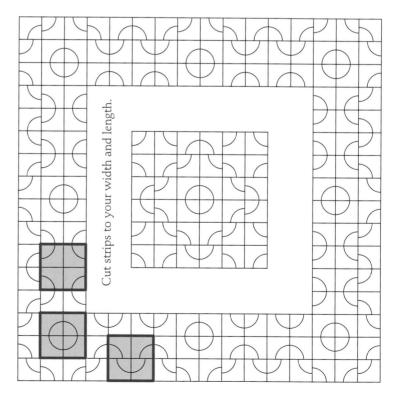

Cut strips to your width and length.

TAPESTRY ROSE

TAPESTRY ROSE
57" x 64"
Made by Elizabeth A. Ballard,
Gaines, Michigan, and
quilted by Susan Myers,
Haslett, Michigan.
3½" template on page 76.

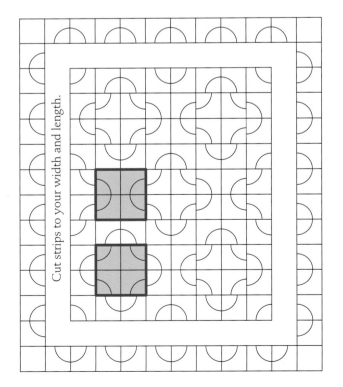

Cut strips to your width and length.

UNCHAINED LINKS

A

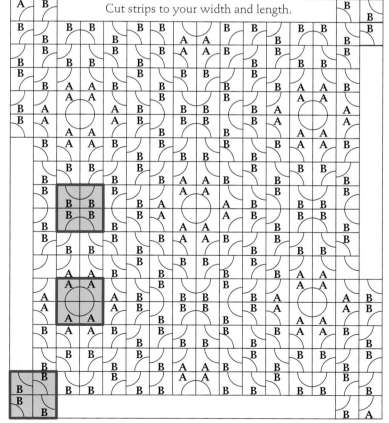

B

UNCHAINED LINKS
64" x 70"
Made and quilted by
Stella Wilcox,
Lake Odessa, Michigan.
4" templates on page 77.

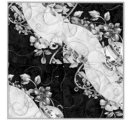

Cut strips to your width and length.

WINTER MEDALLION

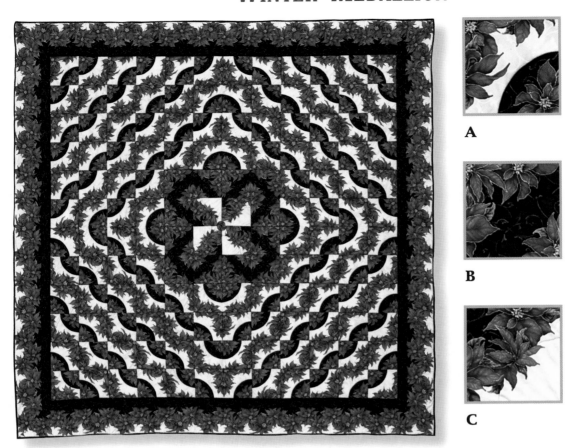

A

B

C

WINTER MEDALLION
72" x 72"
Made by Margaret Metler,
Haslett, Michigan, and
quilted by Susan Myers,
Haslett, Michigan.
5" templates on page 74.

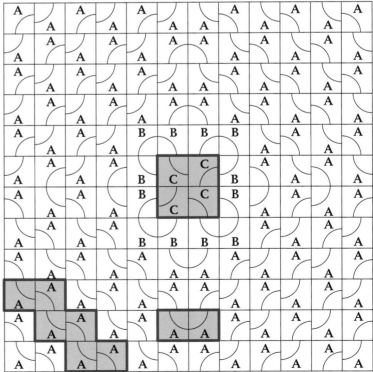

Templates

All sizes indicate the finished block size.

Reminder: Choose the template size based on your fabric. See 1-Fabric Quilt Shopping and Preparations for more information.

Solid lines are cutting lines; dashed lines are sewing lines.

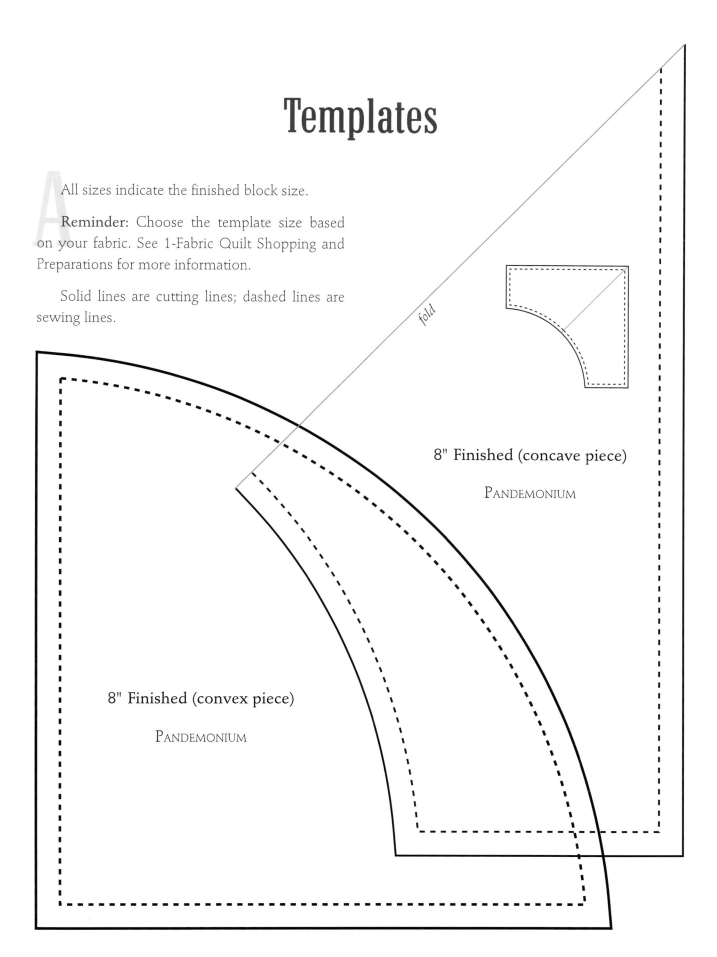

fold

8" Finished (concave piece)

PANDEMONIUM

8" Finished (convex piece)

PANDEMONIUM

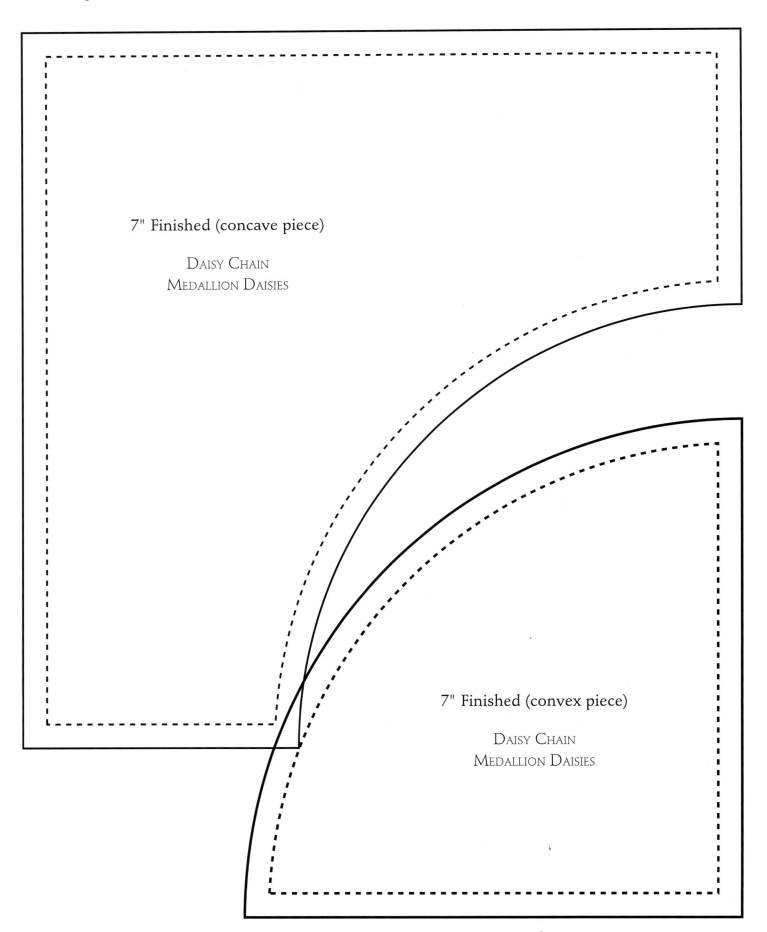

7" Finished (concave piece)

DAISY CHAIN
MEDALLION DAISIES

7" Finished (convex piece)

DAISY CHAIN
MEDALLION DAISIES

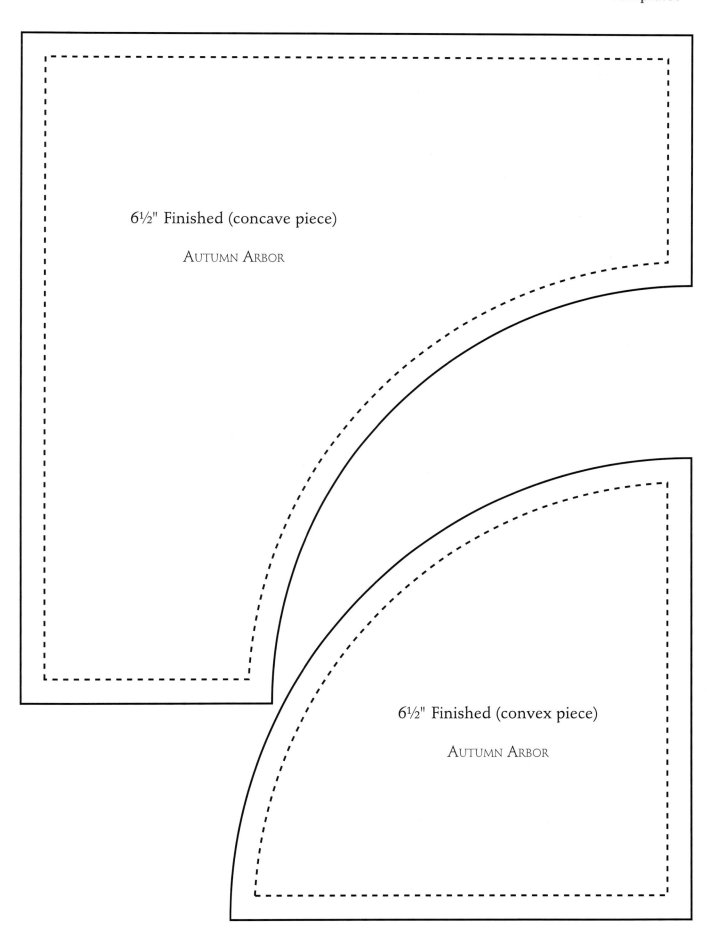

6½" Finished (concave piece)

AUTUMN ARBOR

6½" Finished (convex piece)

AUTUMN ARBOR

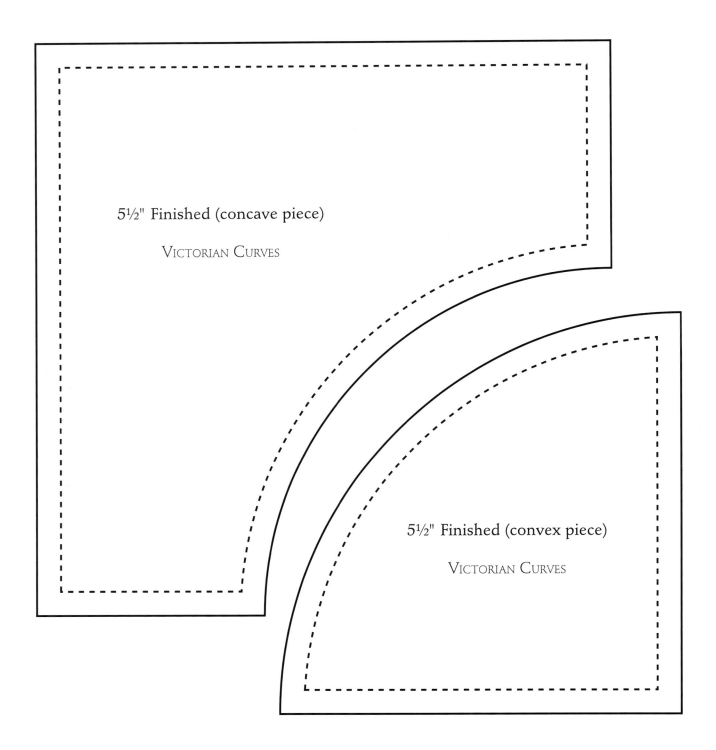

5½" Finished (concave piece)

Victorian Curves

5½" Finished (convex piece)

Victorian Curves

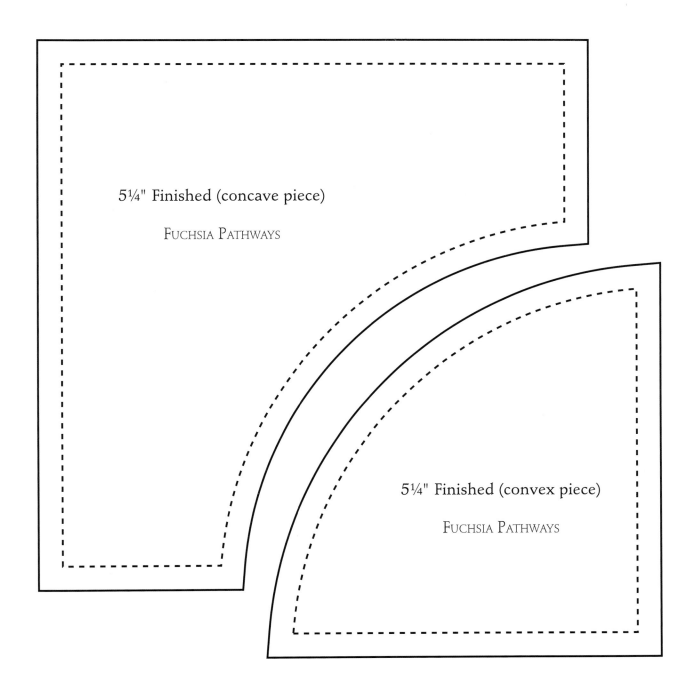

5¼" Finished (concave piece)

FUCHSIA PATHWAYS

5¼" Finished (convex piece)

FUCHSIA PATHWAYS

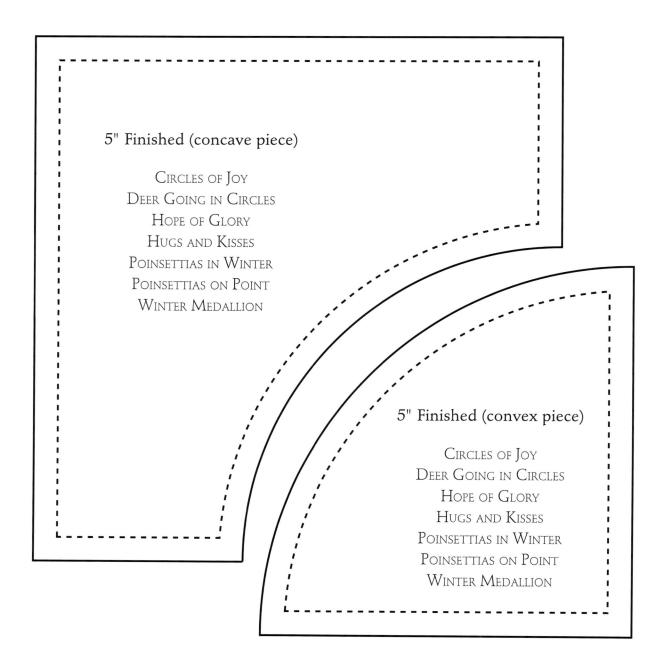

5" Finished (concave piece)

CIRCLES OF JOY
DEER GOING IN CIRCLES
HOPE OF GLORY
HUGS AND KISSES
POINSETTIAS IN WINTER
POINSETTIAS ON POINT
WINTER MEDALLION

5" Finished (convex piece)

CIRCLES OF JOY
DEER GOING IN CIRCLES
HOPE OF GLORY
HUGS AND KISSES
POINSETTIAS IN WINTER
POINSETTIAS ON POINT
WINTER MEDALLION

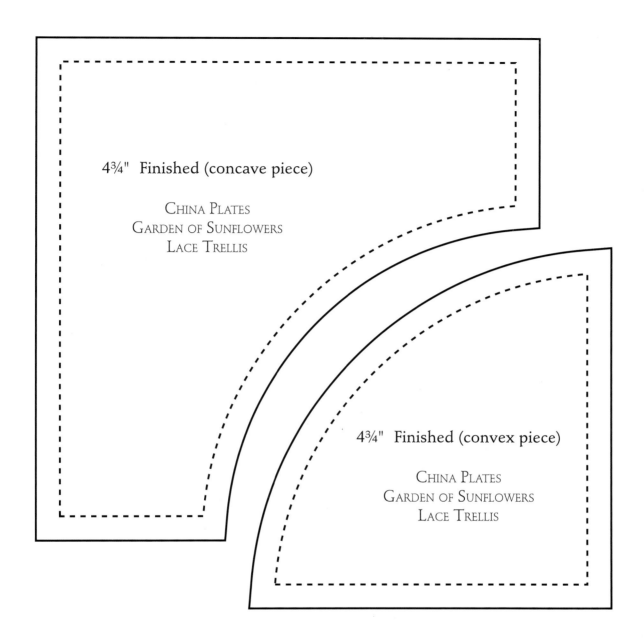

4¾" Finished (concave piece)

CHINA PLATES
GARDEN OF SUNFLOWERS
LACE TRELLIS

4¾" Finished (convex piece)

CHINA PLATES
GARDEN OF SUNFLOWERS
LACE TRELLIS

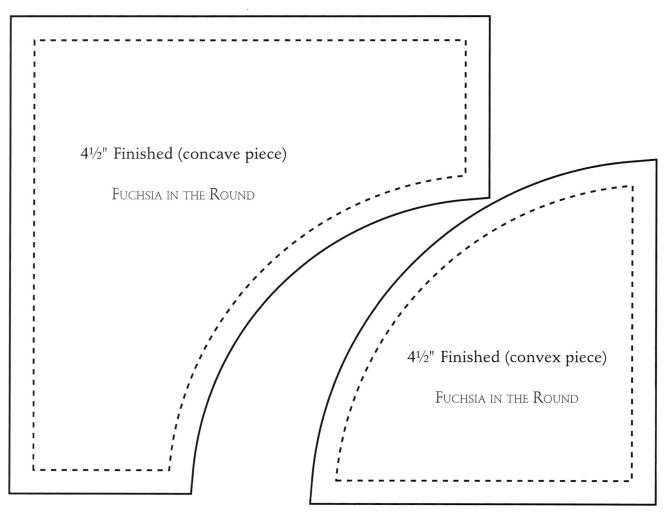

4½" Finished (concave piece)

FUCHSIA IN THE ROUND

4½" Finished (convex piece)

FUCHSIA IN THE ROUND

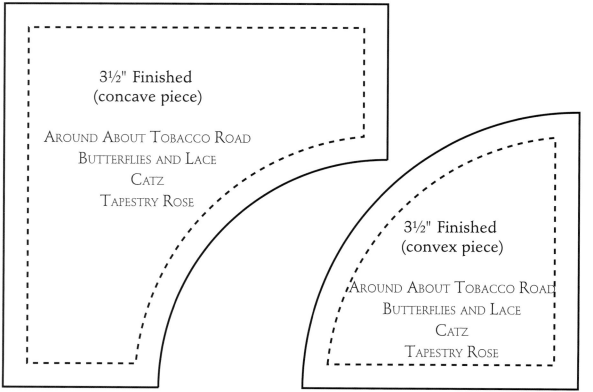

3½" Finished
(concave piece)

AROUND ABOUT TOBACCO ROAD
BUTTERFLIES AND LACE
CATZ
TAPESTRY ROSE

3½" Finished
(convex piece)

AROUND ABOUT TOBACCO ROAD
BUTTERFLIES AND LACE
CATZ
TAPESTRY ROSE

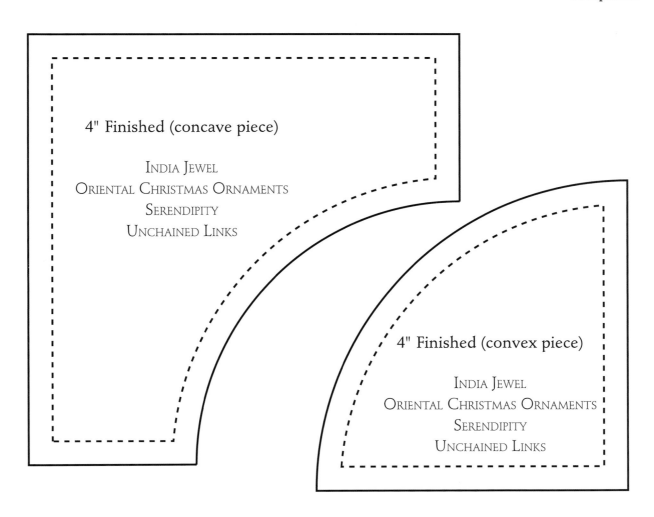

4" Finished (concave piece)

INDIA JEWEL
ORIENTAL CHRISTMAS ORNAMENTS
SERENDIPITY
UNCHAINED LINKS

4" Finished (convex piece)

INDIA JEWEL
ORIENTAL CHRISTMAS ORNAMENTS
SERENDIPITY
UNCHAINED LINKS

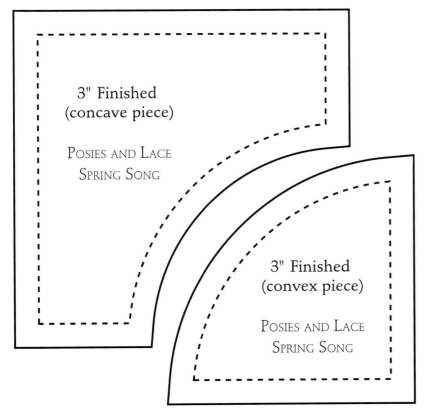

3" Finished
(concave piece)

POSIES AND LACE
SPRING SONG

3" Finished
(convex piece)

POSIES AND LACE
SPRING SONG

Resources / Bibliography

Benartex, Inc.
www.benartex.com

Blank Textiles
www.blankquilting.com

Creative Curves
Virginia A. Walton
www.creativecurves.com

Lyndhurst Studio
www.lyndhurststudio.com

Maywood Studio
Jackie Robinson, Designer
www.animasquilts.com
www.maywoodstudio.com

Northcott
www.northcott.com

Red Rooster Fabrics
www.redroosterfabrics.com

RJR Fashion Fabrics
Jinny Beyer, Designer
www.jinnybeyer.com
www.rjrfabrics.com

South Sea Imports
www.southseafabrics.com

Timeless Treasures
www.ttfabrics.com

Downy® Wrinkle Releaser
www.downywrinklereleaser.
com

Malone, Maggie. *5,500 Quilt Block Designs.* New York, NY: Sterling Publishing Co., Inc.: 2003.

Nickols, Kay. *Wonderful 1 Fabric Quilts.* Paducah, KY: American Quilter's Society: 2007.

About the Author

Kay has become a quilt wrangler and road warrior since the publication of her popular book, *Wonderful 1 Fabric Quilts* (AQS, 2007). She thoroughly enjoys showing beautiful 1-fabric quilts to quilt guilds around the country.

A former schoolteacher, Kay is an enthusiastic instructor who motivates quilters to further develop their creativity and sew unique one-of-a-kind quilts. Students never cease to be amazed at their results by using just one fabric to make a quilt of beauty. Kay teaches a variety of classes from beginning quilting to precision piecing. She has had the opportunity to take classes with national and international quilt instructors who have further enhanced her skill base and teaching ability.

Her quilts have been juried into a number of prestigious international quilt shows and exhibited in shows at the Michigan Women's Historical Center and Hall of Fame in Lansing, Michigan.

Kay is committed to supporting quilt guilds in Michigan. She is an active member of Capital City Quilt Guild, Lansing Area Patchers, Shiawassee Quilters, the Saginaw Piecemakers, West Michigan Quilt Guild, and Michigan Quilt Network (MQN). She and her husband, Rollie, live in Laingsburg, Michigan. Learn more at: http://kaynickols.com/index.html.

THIS PAGE AND OPPOSITE: VICTORIAN CURVES, detail. Full quilt on pages 44.

more AQS Books

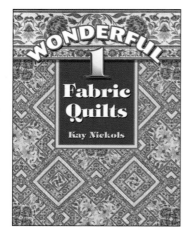

#7487

#8349

#8351

#8350

#8346

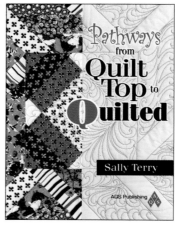

#8348

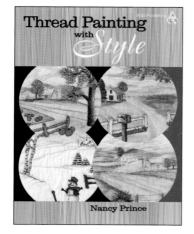

#8354

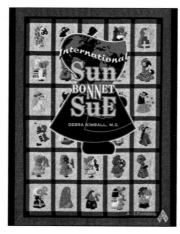

#8347

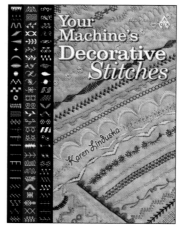

#8353